Defeating Addictions

and Life-Controlling Problems

Luis Torres

PALADIN
PUBLISHING

Defeating Addictions and Life-Controlling Problems
ISBN 978-1-7360332-5-8
Copyright © 2022 by Luis Torres

Published by Paladin Publishing
P. O. Box 700515
Tulsa, OK 74170

Text Design: Lisa Simpson

ENDORSEMENTS

My Friend Luis Torres has a voice that must be heard. His dramatic conversion from drug addiction and substance abuse qualifies him to be an apostolic influence and spiritual father to this generation that is drowning in a sea of illegal and prescription drugs. He has an evident anointing on his life and I believe this is his hour to set the captives free!

**John Kilpatrick, senior founder
and executive pastor
Church of His Presence (AL)
Pastoral oversight of Brownsville Revival in
Pensacola, Florida**

I first met Luis Torres at different gatherings, usually church-related, around town but didn't really know him. I knew he was somehow associated with and was a product of a program called "Teen Challenge."

As a prosecutor, I had had no interaction with that group. However, I was approached to allow a 44-year-old serious drug dealer/user, who was a part of the worst group around, to attend Teen Challenge in order to get probation. Luis Torres convinced me that this would be a good thing. However, I knew the man was destined to fail based upon his history. Plus, he wasn't a teenager.

Well, he not only didn't fail, but excelled in the program and is a success story I refer to today almost 20 years later.

This was the first success story for me working with Luis Torres and this group, but it certainly wasn't the last. Torres has continued to interact with troubled and misguided people within and outside of the criminal justice arena and has continued to have a positive impact on the lives of many.

He has a heart for Jesus and those who need Jesus in their lives. His dedication and resolve seem never to wane.

**Max Cook District Attorney,
Creek County, Oklahoma**

Endorsements

I have been blessed to know Luis Torres for twenty years and counting. Our families have spent time together as we watched our sons playing sports and then successfully pursue their careers. He is anointed to minister to those struggling with addictions and has been faithful to his calling in helping literally thousands overcome substance abuse.

He helped my daughter get free from drugs over twelve years ago. She remains free. She is now a Certified Addiction Counselor and an entertainment tour manager, always helping others.

I encourage you to read this book, *Defeating Addictions and Life-Controlling Problems.* It will give you a new understanding and ability on how to deal with these very pressing problems. He is a pro.

Bobby Daniel, DO, FACOFP

We both have witnessed Pastor Torres minister in prisons, crusades, churches, and on television where many were delivered. He has been an advocate, friend, and counselor to many involved in drug abuse, their families, and those in prison.

This book is greatly needed. It is another manifestation of fruit of a man in pursuit of Jesus Christ, empowered by His Holy Spirit and with zeal to set people free to a life of faith and freedom.

Kent Glesener, President
Paradigm Construction and
Engineering, Inc
Christie Glesener, President
Shofar International Foundation

TABLE OF CONTENTS

INTRODUCTION

I was regularly beaten from the age of three-and-a-half years old. And by the time I reached age nine, my heart had turned to stone after a severely abusive episode. I had already attempted suicide and failed, but at that young age I had no hope.

I was one of nineteen children born to witchcraft-practicing parents in Puerto Rico. Let me just say that bloodshed and mayhem were common occurrences in my life. I suffered severe physical and mental abuse at their hands, and at one time was declared a "son of Satan" by my own mother while she was in a spiritual trance.

When I was fifteen, my father sent me to live with my older brother in New York City. I was filled with anger and rage and soon left my brother to take my chances on the streets. I turned to gang life where I rose to the ranks of warlord for a Brooklyn street gang known as the Mau Maus. I also turned to alcohol and drugs. I should have died as many of my friends did. Instead, I found the power of God which transformed me from the inside out. As I turned my life over to Him, I was delivered from the endless cycle of violence and drug abuse—all by the power of God.

My friend, Luis Torres, has walked through his own horror growing up a loser and the product of a broken family. Like mine, they were caught up in witchcraft, a cocoon of despair and hopelessness. It was true that Luis was "destined for hell" as his biography declares, except for the divine intervention of a powerful, loving God.

I hope this book not only grabs your attention, but changes your life—as God changed ours. And through these insights, may you have your own divine encounter with the power of the living God.

Nicky Cruz – best-selling author
and evangelist

ADDICTIONS

In 2014, one of the most listened to young idols in America, Justin Bieber, was arrested for DUI, drugs, driving with a suspended license, and then taken into custody in Miami, Florida. It wasn't his first run-in with the law regarding substance abuse. Bieber was immediately bonded out of jail by his father, but that very same evening was again seen partying, this time *with his father*.

By the time he reached twenty, Bieber had gotten into almost every type of trouble you can imagine. Since then, he admitted to doing "pretty heavy drugs."[1] With all the pop star had going for him, he got caught in life-controlling addictions. Like many people, he came from a self-described dysfunctional family and battled depression. He turned to drugs and alcohol as his coping mechanisms. But instead of coping, the addictions became controlling.

Substance abuse has grown across the U.S. as young and old alike have turned to drugs, alcohol, etc. especially through the pandemic as many were isolated at home and fell into a downward spiral of depression, fear, and hopelessness. But the Word of God tells us, *"Let not your hearts be troubled. . . . ."*[2]

According to a study by the American Addictions Center:

- 1 in 11 young adults is a heavy drinker (binge drinking on 5 or more days in the past 30 days.)

- 1 in 10 young adults has an alcohol use disorder.

- 1 in 7 young adults has a substance use disorder.

- 1 in 13 young adults has an illicit drug use disorder.

- 1 in 17 young adults has a marijuana use disorder.

- 1 in 100 young adults has an opioid use disorder.[3]

As a former heroin addict facing prison time, I understand the pull and the toll of these life-controlling substances. Addictions affect not only the substance abuser but also their families and friends. And the results are most often devastating.

I am grieved in my spirit not only because of the condition of our nation, but also because of the substance abuse that is plaguing millions of people in America today. The increasingly easy access to prescription drugs, alcohol, tobacco, cocaine, marijuana, Fentanyl, etc. is destroying lives and families.

Addictions today are common not only in America, but in every nation, race, culture, and economic status. Even our military, after they come back from war, are often plagued with physical issues or memories which require prescription drugs in order to cope. The unfortunate thing is that those who get on prescription drugs sometimes begin to abuse them because they want to escape the reality of what is going on in our country.

Addictions are common not only to people who are in low-income housing or minimum wage earners. It can also be found in people who are in professional fields and considered the upper class of society who also get caught in this vicious cycle.

Anything which controls or rules you is your master. Scripture says, *"I am the Lord your God who brought you out of the land of Egypt, out of the house of bondage. You shall have no other gods before Me."*[4] God does not want us to trust in the world's system or substances, but to put our trust in Him.

I have personally been down that road of addiction. For five years I was addicted to heroin. I had a $3,000 a month drug habit—$100 a day. I went to psychiatrists and rehabilitation programs. I was incarcerated for a number of weeks between court cases. I desperately tried to shake that "monkey" of addiction off my back, but with no success. I have watched in horror as these substances are being legalized and brought into our nation at an increasing rate. I feel I must speak out.

A popular drug now legalized in many of our states is marijuana. Although labeled "harmless," it is anything but that. It is an entry point into the world of substance abuse. At first, if you wanted to smoke marijuana, many people were going to Colorado. But now in my own state of Oklahoma, once medical marijuana was legalized, the very next day they began a push for recreational marijuana. Oklahoma now has more licenses for growing marijuana than any other state and not surprising, addictions are skyrocketing as well.

But let me tell you something about marijuana. Marijuana alters the normal communication between cells and circuits in the brain causing poor memory, reduced short-memory function, and diminished brain function overall. Many who are smokers of marijuana do not understand that it can also cause bronchitis.

Now a number of states are trying to legalize marijuana. But every time a person uses something that God did not design for us to use, our immune system is compromised and as a result, because our immune system is compromised, our mind can become a target of Satan. Now here's what the Word of the Lord says in Scripture *"Peace I leave with you; my peace I give you. I do not give to you as the world gives. Do not let your hearts be troubled and do not be afraid."*[5] In verse 6 of this same chapter Jesus says, *"I am the way and the truth and the life. No one comes to the Father except through me."*[6] In Isaiah we are told, *"You will keep in perfect peace those whose minds are steadfast, because they trust in you. . . ."*[7]

I need to also say that a first cousin to using life-controlling substances is prison. We cannot build prisons fast enough to hold the number of people who have broken the law. According to the Prison Policy Initiative, one out of five prisoners have been incarcerated for a drug offense, and on any given day there are 450,000 people arrested for nonviolent drug offenses.[8] Prison construction is one of the fastest-growing industries today. The quicker they build them, the faster they are occupied.

Right now, I serve on a Community Service Board in one of our counties in Oklahoma. I have judges and district attorneys who call me asking for my advice regarding the growing issue of drug use in our nation and how we can slow the spread. One day I asked them why they wanted a preacher, a minister, on their board. They said it was because although they had tried many different options to help those who have become addicted to drugs, they realized they were not working. They hoped to find something that *would* work and came to the church looking for answers.

If you are a drug user, or a family member of a drug user, you need to understand, my friend, the danger of this path. Please stay with me as we look at the many substances now readily available.

The first is the number three killer of people in America. It is prescription drugs.

2

PRESCRIPTION DRUGS

One of the fastest growing industries in America is the pharmaceutical industry, which is prescription drugs. It is the nation's fastest growing drug problem that we face today. This includes prescription narcotics such as OxyContin®. Most often, people who become addicted to OxyContin isn't because it was prescribed for them, but because they have taken it from family or they get them from friends. According to the National Institute on Drug Abuse, over 67 percent of 12th graders who abused prescription narcotics, such as Vicodin® or OxyContin®, were given the drugs by a friend or relative.[9]

Fifty-five percent of emergency room visits involving underaged children was a result of prescription meds left exposed. It is very, very alarming that these prescription drugs are killing so many people. Prescription drugs affect our central nervous system often resulting in another prescription such as Valium to treat the anxiety and side effects caused by the prescription drugs. Drugs like Xanax, Ritalin, and other stimulants are prescribed to keep people "up," which results in anxiety and sleeplessness which requires other pills to bring them back down.

Our over-dependence on prescription drugs is killing people when they are either misused or abused. People sometimes don't even need what they have been prescribed. Remember the verse, *"He shall keep your mind in perfect peace whose mind is stayed on Him?"*[10] Our mind has to become totally surrendered to the Lord because if our mind is not surrendered to the Lord, then we are going to surrender our mind to substances. These will then cause us to put our confidence in mood-altering medications and drugs which have side effects and reactions.

When these reactions hit the human mind, they cause people to do things that often they cannot remember later.

Another very popular pain drug that is prescribed to millions of people all across our nation is Lortab. It is a combination of acetaminophen and hydrocodone.

Hydrocodone is an opioid pain medication that is a narcotic. When abused and misused, it causes addiction. This drug is commonly used for treating moderate and severe pain. Withdrawing from Lortab can result in shallow breathing and even panic attacks. I'll tell you how strong these pills are from personal experience.

I had never used Lortab until I had some issues recently after a root canal. After the procedure, I had excruciating pain to which my dentist prescribed Lortab. I went to the pharmacy and got my prescription filled. There were twelve tablets in the bottle, but because of my knowledge and experience in the past with drugs, I knew that this could be a dangerous situation.

I began to think about what I have believed through the years, that I can do all things through Christ who strengthens me in Philippians 4:13. I realized that I needed to trust God and forge ahead. I went to the bathroom and took one tablet because I was in such discomfort. Later that night, I took a second one, but as I did I thanked the Lord for healing me and asked Him to help me. There were ten Lortab left in the bottle. The next morning, I flushed them down the toilet because I did not want to have that kind of bondage hanging on me.

Here's what God tells you in His Word. *"No weapon that is formed against you shall prosper."*[11] See, the enemy could use that dependency as a stronghold because the more that we use these drugs and narcotics—even when prescribed for us—they can be misused. When we begin to depend upon them, our body begins to build a tolerance to them. Then where it took one pill to see an effect, now it takes two pills, then three pills, and that is when the addiction begins. That is a big problem that we face in America today.

So I warn you and I challenge you, especially parents right now who have children. Most of the arrests today that are taking place among teenagers are kids who are using these pain killers such as Lortab, Xanax, and OxyContin. Parents have come to me because these pills are totally controlling their kids. These prescription drugs are devastating many of our youth today. But I'm here to tell you that God's power and anointing can break that bondage off of them.

I want to once again drive home this scripture into your mind, not only as a parent, but if you are the substance abuser hooked on Lortab, OxyContin, or Xanax and don't know what to do. Let me drill this into your spirit: *"You can do all things through Christ who strengthens you.*"[12] God will strengthen you to fight the battle. The prayer of faith can deliver you and set you free.

Here's what God says: *"When your heart is troubled, bring it to the Lord. For He told, even the disciples, 'Let not your heart be troubled. Neither let it be afraid.'"*[13] The Bible tells us, *"God has not given you the spirit of fear."*[14] Instead, He has given you the spirit of love, power, and a sound mind. God wants you to have a sound mind, so that is why we must keep our minds set on Him.

I want to tell you what I believe is God's prescription for your life. First, it is His Word, which is *"a lamp unto our feet and a light unto our pathway."*[15] He promises us, *"This book of the law shall not depart from your mouth, but you shall meditate in it day and night, that you may observe to do according to all that is written in it. For then you will make your way prosperous, and then you will have good success.*[16] That is His promise, His covenant with us, and He is not going to break His covenant. It will always be with us.

Remember the promise where He tells us, *"In my Father's house are many mansions; if it were not so, I would have told you. I go to prepare a place for you . . . and where I am, you may be also. And if I go prepare a place for you, I will take you in and I'll receive you unto myself."*[15]

ALCOHOL

Alcohol is another devastating killer and life-controlling drug in our nation today. I want to tell you a story about a thirty-three-year-old man in the city where I live. He was a drinker and had been drinking for many, many years. One night he was at a local bar and became intoxicated. When people get drunk, they begin to act foolish, different, out of control. This man got into an argument with a couple of other people who were drinking, and they began to slap him around. He got so upset over how they had treated him that he walked home a few blocks, got his car, and came back with a weapon. As he drove into the parking lot of the bar, he saw the man who had beat him up exiting the bar. Intoxicated, he simply reacted to the rage within him. He ran over his attacker and pinned this man's body against a post.

As the chaplain for the criminal justice system in my city, I was called to talk to this young man just four hours later. He had no clue of what he had done. He did not remember leaving the bar. He did not remember going home and getting in his car. He didn't remember ramming his car into the man and killing him. He sat in the jail cell as I talked to him and repeatedly said, "I do not remember that. I did not do that." Alcohol had taken control of his mind and actions, and the result was a tragedy for both lives. One man was dead and the other's destiny was forfeited because he was controlled and under the influence of alcohol.

When people are under the influence of alcohol it affects their brain and responses. They lose control of their muscles, their speech, and their judgment is altered. Each year thousands are killed in car accidents as a result of a drunk driver.

An .08 percent blood alcohol level is the legal alcohol limit for drivers who are aged 21 and over. Here are some sobering statistics regarding those who have allowed alcohol to control them:

- Drivers with a blood alcohol content over 0.10 are seven times more likely to be involved in a fatal accident than sober drivers.[16]

- According to the National Highway Traffic Safety Administration:

  o one person dies in the U.S. every 50 minutes from drunk driving.

  o Drunk-driving crashes are the reason for more than 10,000 deaths each year.

  o Drinking and driving were to blame for nearly 30 percent of all traffic-related deaths.

  o More than 230 children aged 14 and under were killed in drunk-driving crashes.[17]

Did you know that high blood alcohol levels can cause cirrhosis of the liver, brain impairment, and brain damage? The individual might go into a coma and even die from a too high level. This is what the beer companies do not advertise! Don't just take my word for it; look at the data of the vehicular homicides and involuntary manslaughter from someone who got behind the wheel and drove.

As the pastor of a church, I deal with people every day, families whose children are addicted to alcohol. It is not uncommon for a family member to come to me and say, "I have a son who has four DUIs." Or, "I have a daughter who has three DUIs." It breaks my heart when I see people lose their families because of this killer.

Here's what the Word of the Lord says: *"Wine is a mocker, strong drink is raging. And whosoever is deceived thereby is not wise."*[18] Scripture says, *"Lest they drink, and forget the law, and pervert the judgment of any of the afflicted.*"[19] Let's look at another scripture: *"The saying of King Lemuel——an inspired utterance his mother taught him. Listen, my son! Listen, son of my womb! Listen, my son, the answer to my prayers! Do not spend your strength on women, your vigor on those who ruin kings. It is not for the kings, Lemuel— it is not for kings to drink wine, not for rulers to crave beer.*"[20] When we read these scriptures, it is amazing how they bring such a light to what is going on today in the culture in which we live.

Some of the biggest problems that America has with alcohol consumption is not just among adults who go to bars to have an occasional drink. But the now commonplace encouragement is for people to "drink responsibly." I realize this is a very touchy subject because there are a lot of people, both Christians and non-Christians, who believe drinking is okay.

However, the Bible teaches us that there is really no such thing as "drinking responsibly." If people really believe that they are going to learn how to drink in a responsible fashion, they are just kidding themselves—especially if someone already has an addiction to alcohol. It is not "responsible" to drink and then get behind the wheel of a car where people put their own life in danger, not to mention the lives of others. All we have to do is look at the number of accidents to realize the fallacy of "drinking responsibly." Statistics reveal that alcohol is now the number one drug problem in America with more than 12 million alcoholics in the U.S.[21]

What's happening in our world is so horrific. When we choose to walk into a bar or walk into a party where alcoholic beverages are being served, it does not serve anybody's purpose, but creates the opportunity for trouble.

Let me give you some more scriptures concerning alcoholic beverages such as wine, whiskey, vodka—the things that people use and then say, "We're going to drink responsibly."

A quotation from Proverbs says, *"Who has woe? Who has sorrow? Who has strife? Who has complaints? Who has needless bruises? Who has bloodshot eyes? Those who linger over wine, who go to sample bowls of mixed wine. Do not gaze at wine when it is red, when it sparkles in the cup, when it goes down smoothly! In the end it bites like a snake and poisons like a viper. Your eyes will see strange sights, and your mind will imagine confusing things. You will be like one sleeping on the high seas, lying on top of the rigging. 'They hit me,' you will say, 'but I'm not hurt! They beat me, but I don't feel it! When will I wake up so I can find another drink?'"*[22]

Are you paying attention, my friend? As long as someone is under the influence of alcohol, they are under bondage. Look again at that last line in verse 35. It basically says, "When I awake, I'm going to go back to it again." That's bondage. It's a killer. Unfortunately, it is destroying thousands of people. I'm so glad that Jesus said we can be free from it. Thank You, Father, that today we have the answer and the answer is, *"Therefore if any man be in Christ, he is a new creature: old things are passed away; behold, all things are become new."*[23]

4

TOBACCO

Though most smokers know the danger associated with smoking, most never believe anything will happen to them. With the emergence of e-cigarettes, which has been touted as a breakthrough for smokers, it is simply a new addiction. And manufacturers target young people with the product by wrapping this deadly substance in popular flavors.

Between November 2016 and August 2019, U.S. e-cigarette sales rose by nearly 300 percent according to the Centers for Disease Control and Prevention. Nearly 20 percent of high schoolers and almost 5 percent of middle schoolers reported using vape products in 2020.[24]

The reality is medical experts tell us that tobacco harms nearly every organ of the body. According to the Center for Disease Control (CDC), smoking leads to disease and disability. Recent studies show "more than sixteen million Americans live with a disease caused by smoking. For every person who dies because of smoking, at least thirty people live with a serious smoking-related illness. Smoking causes cancer, heart disease, stroke, lung diseases, diabetes, and chronic obstructive pulmonary disease (COPD), which includes emphysema and chronic bronchitis. Smoking also increases the risk for tuberculosis, certain eye diseases, and problems of the immune system, including rheumatoid arthritis."[25]

Let's think about that. Tobacco use causes disease and reduces the health and longevity in the years of the smoker. And then what about second-hand smoke, which is said to contribute to approximately 41,000 deaths among nonsmoking adults and 400 deaths in infants each year and causes stroke, lung cancer, and coronary heart disease in adults. Also, children who are exposed to second-hand smoke are at increased risk for sudden infant death syndrome and acute respiratory infections.[26]

Your family doctor will tell you about the effects of tobacco on your physical body as it compromises the immune system. It has been the cause of larynx cancer, lung cancer, esophagus cancer, chronic bronchitis, emphysema, gum infections, and more. There is a lot that can be said about this addiction, but the record number of deaths due to tobacco speaks for itself.

Did you know that we have two billion people worldwide who are smokers, and every day 2,800 more people become addicted and join their ranks?

What does the Word of the Lord say about this? Scripture says, *"Do you not know that your bodies are temples of the Holy Spirit, who is in you, whom you have received from God? You are not your own; you were bought at a price. Therefore honor God with your bodies.*[27] Another scripture says, *"For everything in the world—the lust of the flesh, the lust of the eyes, and the pride of life—comes not from the Father but from the world."*[28]

Scripture also says, *"Dear friends, I urge you, as foreigners and exiles, to abstain from sinful desires, which wage war against your soul."*[29]

My word of advice is, if you've never smoked or used other tobacco products or e-cigarettes . . . don't start!

METH

Just the other day, a member of my church came to me concerning a grandson. I have many members, friends, and partners of our ministries who come to us for prayer. This particular problem is almost epidemic. It's methamphetamines.

Meth can cause significant changes to the brain. Some of these changes are immediate and some happen over time. Side effects can include delusions, hallucinations, and depression. But the most common side effect of methamphetamine is paranoia accompanied by uncontrollable movements of the body.

I have been called to the county jail as a chaplain and minister when inmates were coming down from Meth. Many were hallucinating and seeing things in the walls and in their cell. As they were coming down off the artificially induced high, their brain activity went crazy and vicious. You see, my friend, as a minister of the Gospel, as a pastor, as your brother, but mostly as your friend, I need to tell you that the devil is trying to take your mind. But we have a greater weapon in the Word of God, which says, *"You are of God, little children, and have overcome them, because He who is in you is greater than he who is in the world."*[30] And then in another scripture we read, *"For whatever is born of God overcomes the world. And this is the victory that has overcome the world—our faith."*[31]

While the effects of Meth on your mind are devastating, let's look at what it does to your body. "Crystal Meth, a form of methamphetamine, is a very dangerous and addictive street drug. Its popularity is due to the euphoric and hallucinogenic effects it produces and to the fact that opioid abusers sometimes will use Crystal Meth as a substitute when opioids become difficult to obtain.

According to doctors, "Crystal Meth can have profoundly negative effects on several organ systems including the brain, lungs, stomach and bowels, mouth, and skin. But some of the most profound toxicity of this drug relates to the cardio-vascular system. Crystal Meth can cause stroke, heart attacks, heart failure, acute coronary syndrome, cardiac arrest, and sudden death."[32]

These are usually associated with chronic use which can be fatal.

Meth also affects outward appearance. A common trait is ugly mouth sores. All you have to do is go on the Internet. Google "Meth user" and you'll see the mouth sores that are a direct result of the use of this drug.

I have also seen this with my own eyes, the acne created as the toxins from the drug escape through the pores. It restricts the blood flow resulting in facial breakup. It can make a twenty-something-year-old look like a forty-five-year-old. It is devastating. You can see pictures of a twenty-one-year-old who has used Meth since they were fifteen. After six years, it aged them so they looked thirty-five. I've seen pictures of a thirty-year-old lady who started using Meth and now looks like she is sixty-five. Let me say this. Users who smoke Meth often have burns on their lips and around their mouth because of the overheated pipes they use and the hot smoke touching their skin. It destroys their looks on the outside as it destroys their body from the inside.

You say, "Pastor Torres, how do people get hooked on something so devastating to them?" One reason is that they associate with the wrong people. Let's see what scripture says about that. *"Do not be misled. Bad company corrupts good character."*[33]

I have been grieved at the number of young people who are being misled by this thing called "Meth." Recently, a twenty-five-year-old young man wanted to make a little extra money to pay some bills met with an ex-convict. The ex-convict, who had warrants out for his arrest, enticed the young man to use his car along with a twenty-one-year-old girl so they could make what seemed to be some quick, easy money. Together the two drove his car to pick up what is called a "shake and bake," which is a portable Meth lab. As they were driving down the road in this Meth lab, they were pulled over by the police. This twenty-five-year-old, who had godly grandparents who attend church on a regular basis, was arrested. Now he is facing a felony for manufacturing Meth and possession of a Meth lab. Why? Because he was deceived by the people to whom he chose to listen. Remember what I just shared how the Word warns us, *"Be not deceived: evil communications corrupt good manners."*[34] And another scripture, *"For all that is in the world, the lust of the flesh, and the lust of the eyes, and the pride of life, is not of the Father but is of the world.*"[35]

Sadly, now this young man faces a felony conviction on his record because of what happened. The good news from this tragic event is that he accepted Jesus Christ as his personal Savior and is going to receive treatment and faith-based help from the Word of God.

The Word of the Lord is our escape in this time of trouble. The Bible tells us, *"But thanks be to God that, though you used to be slaves of sin, you have come to obey from your heart, the pattern of teaching that has now claimed your allegiance. You have been set free from sin and now have become slaves to righteousness."*[36] If you think you can play with these life-controlling substances and remain in control, you are only fooling yourself. Scripture says, *"Can a man scoop fire into his lap without his clothes being burned?"*[37] You don't control it; it controls you. So, what's the answer? It's found in scripture: *"This I say then, Walk in the Spirit, and ye shall not fulfill the lust of the flesh."*[38] God never said we wouldn't have lust or desire of the flesh. What He said is that when we walk in the Spirit we wouldn't fulfill lust or the desires of the flesh. So my admonition is to walk in the Spirit. Don't become a victim to Meth and allow it to steal your life.

6

FETANYL

Drugs show no favoritism. They kill the rich and poor, male and female alike. Numerous celebrities have fallen into the trap of these addictive substances, such as Fentanyl, opioids, and other strong medications.

1. Prince: Rogers Nelson, American Singer, songwriter, musician, and actor: dead at 57 years old. Cause of death: Fentanyl and Morphine.

2. Michael Jackson: Dead at 50 years old. Cause of death: acute Propofol and Benzodiazepine intoxication.

3. Whitney Houston: Dead at 48 years old. Cause of death: Cocaine, heart disease, drowning.

4. Elvis Presley: Dead at 42 years old. Cause of death: Officially attributed to cardiac arrhythmia, but toxicology results identified 14 drugs in his system, including Codeine, Methaqualone, Morphine, Meperidine, Ethchlorvynol, Diazepam, and Barbiturates.

5. Heath Ledger: Movie star and Actor (The Dark Knight, Patriot, and many more). Dead at 28 years old. Cause of Death: acute intoxication by combined effects of OxyCodone, Hydrocodone,

Diazepam, Temazepam, Alprazolam, and Doxylamine.

6. Judy Garland: Actress, singer, and dancer (Dorothy in "The Wizard of Oz") Dead at 47 years old. Cause of death: Barbiturate overdose.

7. John Belushi: Actor, musician, and comedian. Dead at 33 years old. Cause of death: Cocaine and Heroin overdose.

8. Janis Joplin: American singer-songwriter, sang Rock-n-Roll, Soul, and the Blues. Dead at 27 years old. Cause of death: Heroin overdose.

Unfortunately, the list of tragic deaths continues like a vicious cycle. More than 93,000 Americans died from a drug overdose in 2021, according to the Centers for Disease Control and Prevention. That number is nearly 30 percent higher than the year before. The drastic increase is blamed on Fentanyl.[39]

Over the last year especially, one of the results of the unsecured border is increased drug trafficking. Of the drugs flooding across our borders, the greatest killer is now Fentanyl. This is a synthetic opioid, which is up to fifty times stronger than Heroin and a hundred times stronger than Morphine. From May 2020 through April 2021, more than 100,000 people died from drug overdoses in the U.S.[40] and the numbers continue to increase.

"New data from the Centers for Disease Control and Prevention indicates that Fentanyl-related deaths in the United States have nearly doubled since 2019. The CDC data was compiled by the group Families Against Fentanyl, and also reveals that the powerful opioid is now the leading killer of American adults ages 18-45, causing more deaths than suicide, COVID-19, and car accidents."[41]

Reports indicate that the amount of Fentanyl coming across our unsecured borders is up 300 percent as the current administration turns a blind eye. In January 2021, the Congressional Research Service stated that China remains a major producer of illegal Fentanyl, which is smuggled into the U.S. by traffickers, often through the mail. It is interesting that China is a major part of supplying this drug to the West. Let's consider that during the mid-1800's China's first Opium War was fueled by the West—primarily Britain and the U.S.—who created the market and the subsequent addictions that ravaged China. Now it is happening in reverse. There is a spiritual issue involved in which America needs to repent for what our country and Britain did to create the opium addictions in China in the 1800's then, and we need to close the door to this killer now.

According to a 2021 report from U.S. Customs and Border Protection, a record 20 million Fentanyl pills were seized nationwide, including more than 9.5 million in Arizona alone," [42] It is so deadly that according to the Drug Enforcement Administration, 1 kilo of Fentanyl can kill 500,000 people, and as little as 2 mg. can be the cause of death of an individual. [43]

7

WHAT IS
THE ANSWER?

This is not just a message to read to see what's going on in people's lives. It is to provide scriptures to give you answers to be able to be delivered from the bondage of addiction. Or if you are a friend or family member of someone caught in these addictions, that it will teach you how to pray and stand for their deliverance.

Why are our governmental leaders not doing anything about the abuse of prescription drugs? Because it is a moneymaker. Someone can get a prescription filled for $65, and then turn around and sell it for a significant profit. Then it falls into the hands of our teenagers or our children who then become drug addicts at an early age. As a result, when they grow up if they marry another user, both of their lives continue the downhill slope. Or if they marry a nonuser, eventually it leads to separation or divorce as the crisis spreads in the home. Do you realize that a large percentage of grandparents today are raising their grandchildren because their children are in bondage to these life-controlling substances which they have turned to because they are unable to handle the pressures of life?

A life-controlling problem is something that masquerades as a solution, but in reality it enslaves. It will get the best of you every time. You say, "What is the answer to that, Pastor Torres?" Well, scripture gives us the answer. *"Life and death are in the power of the tongue, and those who love it will eat its fruit."*[44] That scripture is more than just a reminder to be cautious with our words. Look at the scripture again, *"Life and death are in the power of the tongue. . . ."* Let's consider that pills go through your tongue. Alcohol goes through your tongue. Tobacco goes through your tongue. Because the Bible is God's Word, it will deliver you. He says in His Word, *"This is the way, walk in it."*[45] He also told us in His Word, *"In Him we live and move and have our being. . . ."*[46] and *"He will keep your mind in perfect peace, whose mind is stayed on Him."*[47] Jesus said in John, *"I have placed before you an open door,* "[48] and the door that He sets before you is a door that welcomes you into the presence of God to receive Jesus Christ as your personal Savior. When you walk through that door, David said in the Psalms, He will be a lamp unto your feet and a light to your pathway.[49] He is what you need. For Him to be your friend, to set you free and give you deliverance from these bondages, whether that is Meth, drugs, alcohol, tobacco, Lortab, Fentanyl, pills, etc.

If you are dependent on it, you are in bondage. It is a trap. But God is saying to you, my friend, there is an answer. *"Submit yourself therefore to God. Resist the devil, and he will flee from you."*[50]

8

YOU CAN BE FREE

I want to pray for you right now. I know there are people reading this who are users. You're hooked and thinking to yourself, "Pastor Torres, I can't get out of this thing. I've tried this, I've tried that. I've tried everything." Let me tell you, yes, you can. I declare to you, YES, YOU CAN! If I was hooked on a $3,000 a month drug habit and God set me free, then He can set you free as well. My prayer is that as you read this, you will make the decision and say, "I am not going to die with a needle in my arm. I'm not going to swallow pills the rest of my life. I'm not going to lose my life through drinking or heart attacks and strokes caused from any of those habits. I'm not going to get behind the wheel of a car and kill somebody because I'm impaired. I was not born for that. It is not my destiny."

I pray for you right now, whoever you are. Whether you are a parent and are just about to give up on your son, your daughter, your grandson, your granddaughter, your friend. Or if you are someone who is hooked on drugs and you don't know what to do, I believe that God let you get this book into your hands because you needed to understand that there is hope!

Wherever you are and whoever you are, if you've never accepted Jesus Christ as your personal Savior, as your Lord, I want you to say this prayer with me. Even if you think you're not good enough, or that God cannot forgive you for what you have done, I want you to know, that is not the way God looks at it. God is not looking at your problem or your past. He is looking at your potential. So, right where you are, I want you to say this prayer with me:

Dear God in Heaven,
Forgive me of my sins. Cleanse me from all unrighteousness. I confess with my mouth and I believe with my heart that God raised Jesus from the dead, and because He did, I know I can be saved. So, Father, take me in. Rid me of this bondage, this desire for substances that are harmful to me. I receive Your peace that passes all understanding.

I know that there is hope that comes only from You. Father, I know that there is a King in Jesus Christ who cannot be dethroned. I understand that there is a power, Lord, in the Kingdom of God which cannot be exhausted. I accept Jesus Christ as my Savior, Lord, and Master. Come live in my heart, and cleanse me from all these desires and habits that are trying to conquer me. I pray this prayer in the name of the Father, the Son, and the Holy Spirit, in Jesus' name.

Now, I want to pray for you,

Father, I am grieved. I am concerned. I am troubled by the many, many multiple thousands and even millions of people who are addicted. Oh, God, when I realize that we in the United States of America represent 6 percent of the world's population, but we consume 65 percent of the world's illegal drugs, it grieves me, Father. I pray right now, as a minister of the Gospel, and as a father, that You would rid this nation of this evil spirit that is penetrating our country and our world. I am grieved when I see young people go to the grave early and die because of substance abuse. I am broken as I watch parents, grandparents, brothers, sisters, aunts, uncles, and cousins literally lose it because of what is happening with their family members. I pray, Lord, that You would take this message of hope that Jesus gave us, and help us to trust it. Take it all around the world. Take it all over so people can understand that there is a power in Jesus Christ that we can attain, that we can go for, in Jesus' holy, blessed, mighty, majestic name. I thank You and I praise You. Amen.

TESTIMONIES

My name is Blake Hagin. I was raised in a minister's family. My great-grandpa was Kenneth E. Hagin. At an early age, I drifted away from the Lord and started experimenting with drugs. After a time, I became addicted to drugs which set me on a downward spiral that led me to commit a crime. I was arrested and ended up serving time in prison. I was only nineteen years old at the time of my arrest and felt my life was over. While I was in the county jail awaiting being sentenced, my grandfather contacted Pastor Luis Torres. Luis came to visit me in jail. He gave me a book and talked to me about his past that was similar to mine and how God delivered him from addiction. He was instrumental in getting me into Adult and Teen Challenge. My time there set me on a new course and changed my life forever.

I did end up going to prison with an eight-year sentence, but while in prison God supernaturally opened the door for me to be a part of a new program in the prison system called Freedom Challenge that was affiliated with Adult and Teen Challenge. I was able to complete the program while in prison and only served a year. God made a way and moved upon the judge's heart, and I was released to serve the remainder of my sentence on probation.

I just graduated from Rhema Bible College and am working full-time for the ministry. I have been so blessed and given opportunities to share my testimony at churches and youth groups across the

U.S. My life has done a complete 180, and I no longer deal with addiction and have been truly set free! I am married to my wife, Hannah, and we are expecting a baby girl in a few weeks. God is faithful, and no problem is too big for Him to help us overcome!

BLAKE'S MOM

As a parent, there is no greater struggle than to watch your child become someone you no longer recognize due to the powerful addiction of drugs. For several years we tried everything possible to get our son, Blake, help. But it was all to no avail. It took a serious situation to begin the path of him coming back and being set free from the bondage that had such a stronghold on him.

Pastor Luis Torres was instrumental in helping Blake get the help he needed.

Through divine intervention, he helped make a way for him to attend Adult and Teen Challenge in San Antonio, Texas, which was the pivotal point in Blakes's life and the beginning of a transformation only God can do! When your situation seems helpless, and trust me, we had many times that it definitely seemed we had lost him for good, but God intervened and brought the right people at the right time to cross his path.

Never give up; always keep your focus on Jesus to be the Waymaker. We have witnessed Him as the Waymaker in Blake's life and now have peace watching the plan of God for Blake unfold.

Blake's mom, Missy Hagin-Pittman

Jacob Alexander

I grew up in the below-average town in Tulsa, Oklahoma. It would be hard to tell from my later actions as a young adult that I grew up in a very lovely home. I had both my parents at all times, regardless of their personal problems. They provided me with everything we needed, and I was raised to love and treat people with common kindness.

However, no home is perfect, and with the problems that were there, I tried to escape with drugs and alcohol. It first started with seeing the people I idolized on television. As I watched people brag and revolve their life around being intoxicated, I figured I'd try it.

Once I did, I couldn't stop.

Everything I did would start or revolve around drinking or even smoking weed.

The more I did it, the more I needed each time.

Around the age of sixteen I started using hard drugs: Cocaine, Ecstasy, Xanax, and acid. It would start with a weekend thing with my close friends. Then it turned into everyday personal usage to manage my emotions or give me a type of self-medication. Then before I knew it, I was introduced to Meth, a drug that has been destroying my family before I could even imagine. Not learning from my family members' mistakes, I slipped into the world of Meth.

It was grimy and loveless—which clashed with my loving heart. Over time I began to be more ruthless and even started committing violent crimes to either pay for my usage or get it for free. I tried to earn respect in the new life I founded for myself and ended up doing many things I won't write about. I became part of a gang and eventually landed in jail.

I was infatuated with new life and didn't want to stop anytime soon. That is until I got slapped in the face with the sobering charge of armed robbery. Caught red-handed, I was contemplating my new life as a convict. It was lonely and dark.

But my family never stopped loving me, and many friends gave me chance after chance. But they couldn't do anything for me, except God Himself.

God knows all things. He even knows if you truly want change in your heart or are just sorry because you got caught. After spending all those months in prison without drugs, my heart began to feel again. With no interference from drugs or alcohol, I became the real me, the happy boy who wanted to help everyone.

God saw that and sent me one of his guardian angels—Luis Torres. I had never heard of him until he showed up to my maximum-security pod. He described to me his plan for me to go to Teen Challenge. It would be a year-long rehab in Texas. I've been to many rehabs, but not like the Teen Challenge in Brenham, Texas. It was no-nonsense, strict, and the director could sense if you truly wanted change. It was the most challenging thing I've ever done. I couldn't fake it. It was during that time that I truly surrendered to the Lord Jesus Christ. That's when all His love latched onto my heart, and my entire life view was changed. All the numbness and hate I felt as a teen and young adult were transformed into love and patience for others. People ask me how I did it, and I give all the glory to God. Amen.

MARK & TRACI ALEXANDER

We thought we had lost our son to drug addiction and the horror and pain that goes with it. We were in fear for our son's life with the way he was living. When he was eighteen years old, he committed a felony crime due to his heavy drug addiction. He was facing many years in prison at his young age. During our son's time in jail, I was told about a minister, Pastor Luis Torres. I immediately called Pastor Torres for help. There was no hesitation from him whatsoever; he immediately took action. He visited and ministered to our son while he was in jail and remained with us. From that time and throughout the whole process, he supported our son and us. By God's grace, our son was allowed to go to Adult and Teen Challenge in Brenham, Texas, for his drug addiction. Our son now has a second chance and a whole different outlook on life, a new beginning. We know and have experienced God's love and mercy, and we are thankful every day for how God used Pastor Torres to intervene in our son's life. We are very appreciative of the valuable work that he does to help change the lives of young people with drug addictions. There are so many that need help.

LANDYN SPRADLING

Like many other addiction stories, mine started when I began to associate myself with people who didn't have my best interest at heart. My addiction started when I was sixteen years old and in high school. I began to dabble in the party scene, smoking marijuana, drinking alcohol, and taking pills. It didn't take long for the drinking and smoking to fade in importance, and I became hooked on the "harder" drugs. Over the next four years, I consumed on average ten to fifteen pain pills a day costing anywhere from $50-$75 a day—every day. The crazy part is, I never thought I had a problem. Again, like many others who have become addicted, I couldn't just stay with taking pills because that high wasn't satisfying me anymore. I tried it all attempting to satisfy this craving I couldn't overcome. One day someone introduced me to Heroin, and I was immediately hooked. Luckily, I only had about three weeks with that drug before I was arrested. I was then court-ordered into a faith-based drug rehabilitation program, Adult & Teen Challenge. After my stay in jail, this is where I would meet Rev. Luis Torres and when God started a miracle in my life.

Fast forward seven years. I am clean and sober, married, a business owner, a proud member of our church, and serving every Sunday and Wednesday—solely because God gave me strength and patience to complete the program along with all the stipulations the state required with my charges. I am proud to say that *all* the charges against me were expunged, which allowed me to leave my past where it belongs and look forward to the future God has given me. God has been so faithful and more than good to me. I owe all my success to God and a family who believes in the power of prayer. I'm not going to tell you the road to recovery was easy because it wasn't. But I will tell you if you put your faith and trust in God and His Word, all the promises He gives you will come to fruition. To sum it all up, God is always good. Recovery, TRUE RECOVERY, comes *only* from our Heavenly Father.

I'm beyond grateful He saw me fit for His mercy and delivered me.

LANDYN'S DAD — KEVAN SPRADLING

As a parent, born and raised in a dynamically faith-fueled and Spirit-filled home, you never think that you will find yourself in a place where your own child is walking down the road of addiction. Then suddenly, Heroin is staring you and your entire family in the face. Addiction and the grip it has on your loved one doesn't just affect you or them; addiction affects the entire family. It can and will stop you dead in your tracks.

One of the hardest realizations for me as a parent was knowing that my own lackadaisical decisions could have contributed to the very path on which Landyn had landed. I watched as my son went from a healthy, church-going, fun-loving young man so full of life, to a person who had become skin and bones. He had no sense of direction or purpose, and was looking at a possible ten-year prison sentence with a felony conviction.

Our friend, Luis Torres, came to get Landyn and take him to where he needed to be to receive the proper structure that his life needed. It was Teen Challenge in San Antonio, Texas. Little did I know that as a young boy in Wright City, Oklahoma, I had felt led to give money that I had saved for an offering to Luis Torres and his ministry. Now, forty-plus years later that would be the very seed that would create the fruit to put my son on a path of healing and deliverance. Today Landyn is the lead drummer in our church, married to his beautiful wife, Devon, and both have successful businesses and are living for the Lord.

The Bible says, *"Train up a child in the way he should go* (teaching him to seek God's wisdom and will for his talents and abilities)*: and when he is old, he will not depart from it."*[51]

God is faithful to His will and purpose for our lives and that of our children. Amen.

LANDYN'S GRANDFATHER — WALT SPRADLING

The Call That No Parent or Grandparent Ever Wants to Receive . . .

The phone rang, and I picked it up. "Pastor, this is the Carter County Sheriff and I hate to call and tell you, but my deputies just arrested your grandson, Landyn, in an undercover drug bust. They have him in a police car and are transporting him to jail as we speak."

As his grandparent, I was stunned and shocked. I felt as if all the breath had just been knocked out of me. My heart was crushed. My mind was racing, trying to regain my composure enough to answer the sheriff. Our family was devastated. How could our precious, wonderful boy become so trapped by the enemy? As a family, we prayed for him with prayers from our broken hearts.

The Oklahoma statute for dealing with the drugs Landyn was involved with had the possibility of a life sentence. I remember asking the sheriff, who happened to be a very close friend, "Would you put me in the cell with my grandson, and let me stay with him for a while?" So that night I stayed in the jail cell with him for a couple of hours. I cannot describe the pain, the loneliness, or the hurt in those heartbreaking moments, but we prayed together and God was there with us.

On Sunday, I called my dear friend, Luis Torres. I first met Luis in Philadelphia, Pennsylvania, at the Teen Challenge Center. He's a man of God who Jesus saved out of the pit of hell. He was then called into the ministry, and for decades now has traveled the world over rescuing young men and women from addiction. God has used Luis in restoring broken lives that others had given up on—precious young people who have no hope. Tens of thousands have now been reached and restored through the ministry of Luis and Gail Torres.

When I told Luis what had happened, he said, "I'll be there at 9:00 a.m. Monday morning." It was a three-hour drive for him to come to where Landyn was in Ardmore, Oklahoma. At 9:00 a.m. he picked Landyn up and transported him to San Antonio, Texas, to the Teen Challenge Center. He drove all day to get him the help that he needed.

At present, Landyn is saved and serving God in our church. He is the drummer for our praise and worship team. He is faithful to God and to our church. He now owns his own business and just recently married a great Christian young woman who also sings on the praise and worship team. God has done great things in his life.

A NOTE FROM THE AUTHOR

We would like to thank you for taking the time to listen to this very important message on defeating life-controlling problems. We invite you to contact us with questions or prayer requests, or if you would like additional copies of this book or copies of Luis' autobiography, *Destined for Hell,* please write to us at Transformation Outreach Ministries, P.O. Box 556, Sapulpa, OK 74067. Please include a $10 donation per copy for each book or CD requested.

We also ask that you prayerfully consider helping us put this book into the hands of many others who are facing life-controlling addictions by making a tax-free donation to Transformation Outreach Ministries. Large quantities of this book are needed, and this is a powerful way to reach out to the hurting. May God bless you for your love and support of this ministry.

Also, if you have enjoyed reading my story . . . or if you have questions about finding and walking in *your* destiny, I would love to talk with you.

Please feel free to contact me via:

E-mail: ltorres@cox.net
Facebook: https://www.facebook.com/
revluistorres
Mail: Transformation Outreach
Ministries, Luis Torres,
P.O. Box 556,
Sapulpa, OK 74067
Website: luistorres.org

ABOUT THE AUTHOR

Luis Torres is a lead pastor in Oklahoma as well as president of Transformation Outreach Ministries. He also serves on the Creek County Community Sentencing Board which oversees drug court, probation and parole.

For additional information go to:
luistorres.org

Endnotes

[1] Caitlin O'Kane, "Justin Bieber Admits to 'Heavy Drug Use,'" CBS News, September 3, 2019, https://www.cbsnews.com/news/justin-bieber-instagram-admits-to-heavy-drug-use-opens-up-about-struggles-with-fame-and-relationships-hailey-baldwin/ Accessed January 11, 2022.

[2] John 14:1 NIV

[3] Editorial Staff, "Alcohol and Drug Abuse Among for Young Adults," American Additions Center, January 2, 2020, https://americanaddictioncenters.org/rehab-guide/addiction-statistics/young-adults   Accessed January 11, 2022.

[4] Exodus 20:2-3 NKJV

[5] John 14:27 NIV

[6] John 14:6 NIV

[7] Isaiah 26: 3 NIV

[8] Prison Policy Initiative, https://www.prisonpolicy.org/graphs/pie2020_drugs.html Accessed January 20, 2022.

[9] National Institute on Drug Abuse, 2012, https://archives.drugabuse.gov/monitoring-future-survey-overview-findings-2012 Accessed January 17, 2022.

[10] See Isaiah 26:3 NIV

[11] See Isaiah 54:17 NKJV

[12] See Philippians 4:13 NKJV

[13] See John 14:2-3 NIV

[14] See 2 Timothy 1:7 NKJV

[15] See Psalm 119:105 NIV

[16] Joshua 1:8 NKJV

[15] See John 14:2-3 NIV

[16] 2018 Drunk Driving Stats Book, Responsibility. org, https://www.responsibility.org/wp-content/uploads/2020/02/2018_Drunk-Driving-Stats-Book.pdf Accessed January 17, 2022.

[17] Lena Borrelli, "2021 Drunk Driving Statistics," MSN Money, Feb. 9, 2021, https://www.msn.com/en-us/money/other/2021-drunk-driving-statistics/ar-BB1dxdXF Accessed January 17, 2022.

[18] Proverbs 20:1 KJV

[19] Proverbs 31:5 KJV

[20] Proverbs 31:1-4 NIV

[21] Kayla Loibl, "Statistics on Alcoholics," Learn About Alcoholism, Sept. 23, 2020, https://www.learn-about-alcoholism.com/statistics-on alcoholics.html#:~:text=It%20is%20an%20alcoholism%20fact%20that%3A%201%20Alcohol,car%20accident%20every%2030%20minutes.%20More%20items...%20 Accessed January 17, 2022.

[22] Proverbs 23:29-35 NIV

[23] 2 Corinthians 5:17 KJV

[24] Lauren Mascarenhas, "FDA Blocks Sale of 55,000 Flavored E-cigarette Products," CNN Health, August 26, 2021, https://www.cnn.com/2021/08/26/health/fda-blocks-ecig-products/index.html Accessed January 17, 2022.

[25] Smoking and Health Effects from Tobacco Use, Centers for Disease Control, https://www.cdc.gov/tobacco/basic_information/health_effects/index.htm Accessed January 17, 2022.

[26] Ibid.

[27] 1 Corinthians 6:19-20 NIV

[28] 1 John 2:16 NIV

[29] 1 Peter 2:11 NIV

[30] 1 John 4:4 NIV

[31] 1 John 5:4 NIV

[32] Maureen Salaman, "Crystal Meth Causes Severe Heart Damage," Very Well Health, July 11, 2020, https://www.verywellhealth.com/crystal-meth-causes-severe-heart-damage-3892537 Accessed January 17, 2022.

[33] 1 Corinthians 15:33 NIV

[34] 1 Corinthians 15:33 KJV

[35] 1 John 2:16 KJV

[36] Romans 6:`17-18 NIV

[37] Proverbs 6:27 NIV

[38] Galatians 5:16 KJV

[39] "Illegal Drug Trade Goes From the Corner to the Web," United States Dept of Justice, October 31, 2021, https://www.justice.gov/opa/blog/usa-today-op-ed-illegal-drug-trade-goes-corner-web-rising-deadly-threat-fake-pills Accessed January 18, 2022.

[40] Zachary B. Wolf, CNN Politics, November 18, 2021, https://www.cnn.com/2021/11/17/politics/

fentanyl_overdose-deaths-what-matters/index.html
Accessed January 4, 2022.
[41] Tim Meads, "Fentanyl Deaths Skyrocket," The Daily Wire, Dec. 17, 2021, https://www.dailywire.com/news/fentanyl-deaths-skyrocket-becoming-nations-leading-killer-for-adults-age-18-45 Accessed January 18, 2022.
[42] "Drug Seizure Statistics," U.S. Customs and Border Protection, Dec. 15, 2021, https://www.cbp.gov/newsroom/stats/drug-seizure-statistics Accessed January 18, 2022.
[43] Tim Meads, "Fentanyl Deaths Skyrocket," The Daily Wire, Dec. 17, 2021, https://www.dailywire.com/news/fentanyl-deaths-skyrocket-becoming-nations-leading-killer-for-adults-age-18-45 Accessed January 18, 2022.
[44] Proverbs 18:21, Holman Christian Standard Bible
[45] Isaiah 30:21 NIV
[46] Acts 17:28 NIV
[47] Isaiah 26:3 paraphrase
[48] Revelation 3:8 NIV
[49] Psalm 119:105
[50] James 4:7 - ESV
[51] Proverbs 22:6 KJV